Belongs to

Letters to my Daughter

Letters to my Daughter

Letters to my Daughter

Letters to my Daughter

Letters to my Daughter

Letters to my Daughter

Letters to my Daughter

Letters to my Daughter

Letters to my Daughter

Letters to my Daughter

Letters to my Daughter

Letters to my Daughter

Letters to my Daughter

Letters to my Daughter

Letters to my Daughter

Letters to my Daughter

Letters to my Daughter

Letters to my Daughter

Letters to my Daughter

Letters to my Daughter

Letters to my Daughter

Letters to my Daughter

Letters to my Daughter

Letters to my Daughter

Letters to my Daughter

Letters to my Daughter

Letters to my Daughter

Letters to my Daughter

Letters to my Daughter

Letters to my Daughter

Letters to my Daughter

Letters to my Daughter

Letters to my Daughter

Letters to my Daughter

Letters to my Daughter

Letters to my Daughter

Letters to my Daughter

Letters to my Daughter

Letters to my Daughter

Letters to my Daughter

Letters to my Daughter

Letters to my Daughter

Letters to my Daughter

Letters to my Daughter

Letters to my Daughter

Letters to my Daughter

Letters to my Daughter

Letters to my Daughter

Letters to my Daughter

Letters to my Daughter

Letters to my Daughter

Letters to my Daughter

Letters to my Daughter

Letters to my Daughter

Letters to my Daughter

Letters to my Daughter

Letters to my Daughter

Letters to my Daughter

Letters to my Daughter

Letters to my Daughter

Letters to my Daughter

Letters to my Daughter

Letters to my Daughter

Letters to my Daughter

Letters to my Daughter

Letters to my Daughter

Letters to my Daughter

....
....
....
....
....
....
....
....
....
....
....
....
....
....
....
....
....
....
....
....
....
....
....
....
....

Letters to my Daughter

Letters to my Daughter

Letters to my Daughter

Letters to my Daughter

Letters to my Daughter

Letters to my Daughter

Letters to my Daughter

Letters to my Daughter

Letters to my Daughter

Letters to my Daughter

Letters to my Daughter

Letters to my Daughter

Letters to my Daughter

Letters to my Daughter

Letters to my Daughter

Letters to my Daughter

Letters to my Daughter

Letters to my Daughter

Letters to my Daughter

Letters to my Daughter

Letters to my Daughter

Letters to my Daughter

Letters to my Daughter

Letters to my Daughter

Letters to my Daughter

Letters to my Daughter

Letters to my Daughter

Letters to my Daughter

Letters to my Daughter

Letters to my Daughter

Letters to my Daughter

Letters to my Daughter

Letters to my Daughter

Letters to my Daughter

Letters to my Daughter

Letters to my Daughter

Letters to my Daughter

Letters to my Daughter

Letters to my Daughter

Letters to my Daughter

Letters to my Daughter

Letters to my Daughter

Letters to my Daughter

Letters to my Daughter

Letters to my Daughter

Letters to my Daughter

Letters to my Daughter

Letters to my Daughter

Letters to my Daughter

Letters to my Daughter

Letters to my Daughter

Letters to my Daughter

Letters to my Daughter

Letters to my Daughter

Letters to my Daughter

Letters to my Daughter

Letters to my Daughter

Letters to my Daughter

Letters to my Daughter

Made in the USA
Monee, IL
12 May 2022

96286250R00075